Pa-PY-rus.   Right, pa-PY-rus.   I like catching yummy flies.   I like listening to Miriam sing!

For P-Quy and Nandocito Carson

Dear Children,

The story of Miriam is from the Bible, Exodus, Chapter 2: Verses 1–10.
I love this story because it is about a brave little girl who helped save her
baby brother. We know from the Bible that Miriam sang as an adult.
When I wrote this book, I wrote songs for her to sing as a child, too. If
you want to sing Miriam's songs (and I hope you will), you can do so to
either the tune of "Hava Nagila" or "You Are My Sunshine."

You might want to share the reading of this story with others. One person
can be the narrator, and others can speak (or sing) the lines of the characters.
Whoever speaks for the fish should go last, just before you turn the page.

Happy singing!
Jean Marzollo

I am deeply grateful for the assistance of
my friend Jill Cohen; agent Molly Friedrich; publisher David Ford;
editor Simone Kaplan; art director Alyssa Morris; Rev. T. Richard Snyder;
Rabbi Stacey Schlein; Betsy Polivy; and Irene Seff. Thanks also to Sheila
Rauch; Mim Galligan; Carol Devine Carson; Shelley Thornton; Patricia
Adams; Irene O'Garden; Sandra Nice; the First Presbyterian Church
of Philipstown; my sons, Daniel and David; my husband,
Claudio; and all the children who tested the book.

First Edition
ISBN 0-316-74131-0
LCCN 2002116719

10 9 8 7 6 5 4 3 2 1

TWP

Printed in Singapore

The illustrations for this book were painted in watercolor, then scanned and finished in Adobe Photoshop on a
Power Mac G4. The text was set in Hadriano Light and Kid Print, and the display type was set in Sand.

A BIBLE STORY
Retold and illustrated by JEAN MARZOLLO

Miriam and Her Brother Moses

LITTLE, BROWN AND COMPANY

New York ∾ An AOL Time Warner Company

Why does Miriam carry a jug of water on her head?　　She has to. She's a slave.　　Carrying water is her job.

Introduction

Miriam lived long, long ago with her family in a country called Egypt, but they were not Egyptians. They were Hebrews originally from the Land of Canaan. Long before Miriam was born, the Hebrews had moved from Canaan. They moved because their food crops had died from lack of rain. In Egypt the crops were green and there was plenty to eat. For many, many years the Egyptians and the Hebrews lived together in peace.

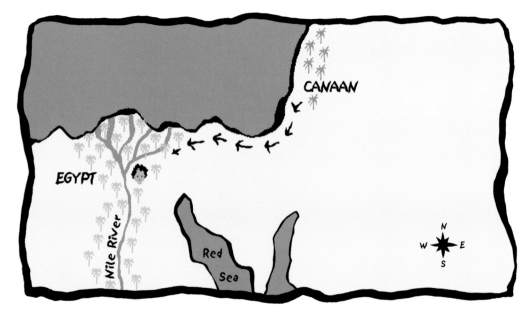

But not in Miriam's time. In Miriam's time a wicked king called Pharaoh forced the Hebrews into slavery. The Hebrew slaves built huge pyramids and temples. They were not paid for their work. All they received was a little food and bad housing. But they had no choice. If they didn't work, they were punished.

Children were slaves, too. Miriam's family worked at an outdoor brick factory. Miriam's job was to carry water from the river to the factory. Her mother mixed the water with clay, sand, and straw. Her father shaped the mixture into bricks, which her brother Aaron set in the sun to dry.

Swim, Little Fishies,
Swim, Little Fishies,
Swim, Little Fishies,
Swim, Little Fish.

Is she singing to us?   Yes!   Why does she sing if she's a slave?   I think singing makes her work a little easier.

The Story: Miriam and Her Brother Moses

Pharaoh was scared. He liked having lots of slaves, but he feared having too many. What if the Hebrew slaves decided to fight his soldiers? And what if the Hebrews won? Pharaoh became so frightened that he gave his soldiers a truly terrible order.

Just after Pharaoh issued his dreadful command, Miriam's mother gave birth to a baby boy. The family hid him from Pharaoh's soldiers by keeping him inside their little mud hut. Miriam helped to keep her baby brother quiet by singing to him in her whisper voice.

Hush, Little Baby,
Hush, Little Baby,
Hush, Little Baby,
Hush, Little Babe.

But every day Baby grew, and the family knew that they couldn't keep him inside and quiet forever. How could they keep Baby safe? Together, the family came up with a plan. They would make Baby a boat and sail him down the river.

Where will the boat take him?   To a place where kind people will find him and care for him.   That's what they're hoping.

To make the boat, Miriam and Aaron picked papyrus reeds from the river's edge. Next, Mother wove the reeds back and forth and back and forth to make a basket.

Mother waterproofed the basket with tar and pitch. At dawn the next morning, she lined it with a soft blanket and put Baby inside. Everyone was afraid, so Miriam sang and danced to keep Baby from catching their fears.

Smile, Little Baby,
Smile, Little Baby,
Smile, Little Baby,
Smile, Little Babe.

Why did she put flowers on the blanket?   Camouflage!   What's that?   You'll see. . . .

Quietly Miriam and her family went to the river. They prayed that Baby would stay asleep and be hidden from the soldiers. Gently, Mother set the basket into the Nile. Then, Miriam's family had to leave for work at the brick factory. If they were late, the soldiers would punish them.

Sleep, Little Baby,
Sleep, Little Baby,
Sleep, Little Baby,
Sleep, Little Babe.

As planned, Miriam followed the basket down the river. She hoped that if the soldiers saw her, they would think that she was just a slave girl fetching water from the river. Miriam kept on singing. So far so good, she thought.

Dream, Little Baby,
Dream, Little Baby,
Dream, Little Baby,
Dream, Little Babe.

The basket matches the papyrus!   Is that camouflage?   Yes.

Quack! Quack! Quack! Ducks flew into the air. Would they wake Baby? No. Baby was still sleeping. But now a soldier was coming! Miriam's heart was pounding. She had to think. She sang out in her sweetest voice and even danced a little on the path. The soldier watched her closely and passed by.

Fly, little duckies,
Fly, little duckies,
Fly, little duckies,
Fly, little ducks.

Quack!

Quack! Quack!

It worked! He never noticed Baby!   That Miriam is clever.   But, uh-oh. I hear more people ahead.

Miriam walked quietly now because she heard something. Just over a little hill, she came upon a rich woman and her maids going down to the river. Oh-no! The rich woman was Pharaoh's daughter, the princess!

The princess saw Baby floating in the river and sent a slave to fetch him. Baby began to cry. **Waa-aaa!** The slave lifted the basket out of the river.

Give him to me.

Waa-aaa!
WAA-AAA!
WAA-AAA!

Will Pharaoh's daughter throw Baby into the river?   I don't think so.   She doesn't look that mean.

Pharaoh's daughter wasn't mean at all. Lifting Baby gently into her arms, she rocked him and made cooing sounds like a dove. When Baby stopped crying, the princess smiled.

Such a sweet little boy! I will raise him as my own and name him Moses, which means, "taken from the water."

The maids were shocked! They knew that Pharaoh would NOT want his daughter to raise a Hebrew baby. But when Miriam saw how loving the princess was, she had an idea. Did she dare tell her idea to Pharaoh's daughter? Yes, she did.

Your highness, would you like me to find a good, kind Hebrew woman who has plenty of milk for . . . Moses?

The princess said yes, so Miriam ran all the way to the brick factory!

Does this mean Moses is safe?   Yes.   Does this mean he was rescued by someone who was taught to hate Hebrews?   Yes!

Miriam brought her mother to the river. There, Pharaoh's daughter handed Moses to her.

The princess had no idea that she was giving Moses back to his real mother and sister, but she saw that Moses was contented, and that made her happy. Happiest of all, though, were Miriam and her mother.

What about Pharaoh?   They don't have to worry about him for three years.

Three years passed quickly. Miriam's father and brother still worked at the brick factory, but Miriam helped her mother take care of Moses in the slave quarters of Pharaoh's palace. Miriam taught him games and songs that she hoped he would remember when he became a prince.

Sing, Little Baby,
Sing, Little Baby,
Sing, Little Baby,
Sing, Little Babe.

From time to time Pharaoh's daughter visited Moses, and she was pleased with the good care he was receiving. On his third birthday she placed a gold necklace around his neck.

The time has come, my son, for you to meet Pharaoh. He is the King of Egypt and your grandfather!

Pharaoh will be furious! He doesn't want a Hebrew grandson!   But the princess is brave.   She's spunky. Like Miriam!

Miriam and her mother followed the princess and Moses to Pharaoh's chambers and watched as they approached Pharaoh on his throne.

Father, this is Moses. He is your grandson. I have adopted him and will raise him as an Egyptian prince.

The palace was quiet. Miriam, her mother, and all the slaves in the palace shut their eyes and prayed. Pharaoh stared at his soldiers, he stared at his daughter, and he stared at Moses. Finally, he spoke.

Miriam and her mother joined the rest of the family at the brick factory. Years passed. Sometimes, as she worked, Miriam would see Moses ride by in a royal chariot driven by one of Pharaoh's soldiers. The soldiers were always nice to him, and Moses seemed very happy.

In time, both Miriam and Moses grew up. The prince drove the chariot alone now. Miriam was sad to think that her brother no longer remembered her.

Does he remember that he is a Hebrew?   He sure doesn't act like it.

Then one hot day, as Miriam was carrying water, she heard chariot wheels—and a strong voice singing a familiar song. The voice came closer and closer. Miriam turned and saw Prince Moses. He was singing to her!

His song told her that Moses DID remember her and all the songs that she had taught him. The look in his eyes told her more. It told her that he wanted to help his family.

Sing, Little Baby,
Sing, Little Baby,
Sing, Little Baby,
Sing, Little Babe.

Suddenly Miriam had a vision. She saw — not with her eyes, but with her heart and mind and soul — that one day her powerful brother would free the Hebrew slaves and lead them out of Egypt. Miriam clapped her hands and sang a new song, one she had never sung before.

Lead, Little Baby,
Lead, Little Baby,
Lead, Little Baby,
Lead, Mighty Prince.

Does Moses really lead the slaves to freedom?   Yes.   Does Miriam help?   Yes! But that's another story!

Let's play hide and seek in the . . . how do you say it?   Pa-PY-rus! Okay, you're it!